TOM BRADY

AND THE NEW ENGLAND PATRIOTS

BY BARRY WILNER

Alameda Free Library
1550 Oak Street
Alameda, CA 94501

SportsZone

An Imprint of Abdo Publishing
abdopublishing.com

abdopublishing.com

Published by Abdo Publishing, a division of ABDO, PO Box 398166, Minneapolis, Minnesota 55439.
Copyright © 2019 by Abdo Consulting Group, Inc. International copyrights reserved in all countries.
No part of this book may be reproduced in any form without written permission from the publisher.
SportsZone™ is a trademark and logo of Abdo Publishing.

Printed in the United States of America, North Mankato, Minnesota
032018
092018

THIS BOOK CONTAINS
RECYCLED MATERIALS

Distributed in paperback by North Star Editions, Inc.

Cover Photo: Paul Spinelli/AP Images, foreground; Al Messerschmidt/AP Images, background
Interior Photos: Ben Liebenberg/AP Images, 4–5; Elise Amendola/AP Images, 6, 13, 43; Greg Trott/AP
Images, 9; Paul Spinelli/AP Images, 10; NFL Photos/AP Images, 14–15; Donald Preston/Boston Globe/AP
Images, 16; Charles Krupa/AP Images, 19; Al Messerschmidt/AP Images, 20–21; Jim Davis/Boston Globe/
AP Images, 23; G. Newman Lowrance/AP Images, 25, 33; Winslow Townson/AP Images, 26; Jim Mahoney/
AP Images, 28–29; Kathy Willens/AP Images, 31; Eric Gay/AP Images, 34; Damian Strohmeyer/AP Images,
37, 38–39; Mary Schwalm/AP Images, 40

Editor: Patrick Donnelly
Series Designer: Craig Hinton

Library of Congress Control Number: 2017962596

Publisher's Cataloging-in-Publication Data

Names: Wilner, Barry, author.
Title: Tom Brady and the New England Patriots / by Barry Wilner.
Description: Minneapolis, Minnesota : Abdo Publishing, 2019. | Series: Sports dynasties | Includes online
    resources and index.
Identifiers: ISBN 9781532114373 (lib.bdg.) | ISBN 9781641852869 (pbk) | ISBN 9781532154201 (ebook)
Subjects: LCSH: Brady, Thomas Edward, Jr., 1977-.--Juvenile literature. | Football players--United States-
    -Biography--Juvenile literature. | Football--Juvenile literature. | New England Patriots (Football
    team)--Juvenile literature.
Classification: DDC 796.332092 [B]--dc23

TABLE OF CONTENTS

CHAPTER 1

THE SUPER COMEBACK

The New England Patriots were done. It was as plain as day. They had no chance. The Patriots trailed the Atlanta Falcons 28–3 deep into the third quarter of the Super Bowl in February 2017. Atlanta's defense had sacked Patriots quarterback Tom Brady twice and forced him into many rushed throws. He even threw an interception that Falcons cornerback Robert Alford returned 82 yards for a touchdown late in the second quarter.

Tom Brady was looking for his fifth Super Bowl ring when he faced the Atlanta Falcons in February 2017.

Robert Alford (23) avoids Brady's attempted tackle as he races to the end zone for a Falcons touchdown.

The image of Brady diving in vain trying to tackle Alford was all over social media.

Meanwhile New England's defense couldn't stop Falcons quarterback Matt Ryan. The league's Most Valuable Player (MVP) that season had thrown for two touchdowns and led some lengthy drives.

Maybe it just wasn't New England's day. In fact, one sportswriter turned to another in the press box and said,

"This game is over." The reply: "Do you know who you are talking about? This is Tom Brady and the Patriots. It's not over."

And it wasn't. Sure, the biggest Super Bowl comeback ever had been just 10 points, which three teams managed. One of those was the Patriots just two years earlier. They trailed Seattle 24–14 and won 28–24.

Many of the Patriots remembered that rally. So when Brady led a 75-yard drive and James White caught a 5-yard touchdown pass late in the third quarter, they gained some confidence.

So did their thousands of fans at NRG Stadium in Houston. Even though Stephen Gostkowski, the top kicker in the National Football League (NFL) that year, missed the extra point, that touchdown showed the Patriots—and maybe even the Falcons—that it was still a game.

FALCONS FADING

New England got the ball back early in the fourth quarter still trailing 28–9. But it soon became clear Atlanta's defense was tiring. Brady was getting more time to throw. That's the last thing you want to give any quarterback, let alone the most successful one of his generation.

But the Falcons sacked Brady, and the Patriots settled for a field goal. Atlanta still led 28–12. Yet the Patriots believed.

"Down 25 points, it's hard to imagine us winning it," Brady said. "When we got rolling there in the second half it was tough to slow us down."

LATE START

Tom Brady missed the first four games of the 2016 season because he was suspended by the NFL. Brady was found to have known about footballs being deflated in the Patriots' win over Indianapolis in the 2014 American Football Conference (AFC) Championship Game. Deflating balls supposedly makes it easier to hold them in cold weather. Brady fought the league in court for more than a year before sitting out the games. New England went 3–1 without him.

"Tough" became downright impossible for the Falcons the next time New England got the ball. Ryan had fumbled at his 25-yard line, by far the biggest defensive play New England

had made. It took only two and a half minutes for the Patriots to score, this time on a 6-yard pass from Brady to Danny Amendola. When White ran in for a two-point conversion, it was 28–20 with just under six minutes to play.

At that point, Brady looked into the crowd and spotted his family. His mother, Galynn, had been seriously ill and didn't go to any games that season. But she was in the stadium for this one. Her son, who rarely needs more of a competitive edge, was even more motivated for this Super Bowl. And Tom Brady felt sure he could win another one for his mom.

His defense, though, would need to come through again. Things looked bleak when Ryan completed a 39-yard pass to Devonta Freeman and a 27-yarder to Julio Jones, putting Atlanta at the New England 22.

Then things got strange. A field goal would likely have put the game out of reach. But the Falcons didn't play it safe. They kept passing. That turned out to be a bad decision. A sack and a holding penalty knocked them out of field goal range, and they decided to punt.

ONE LAST SHOT

With three and a half minutes left, New England got the ball at its 9-yard line. Atlanta's defense was exhausted. The Patriots didn't have a lot of time, but it was more than enough for Brady.

Julian Edelman made a sensational catch on Brady's desperate heave to get the Patriots to midfield. Four plays later, with 57 seconds to go, White strolled into the end zone from a yard out. Amendola got free in the end zone for the two-point conversion pass to tie it at 28.

By that point there was little doubt that New England would win. When the Patriots won the coin toss to start overtime, it took Brady just nine plays to cover 75 yards. White's third touchdown, a 2-yard run that gave him a record 20 points in a Super Bowl, set off a wild celebration.

"It was just a lot of mental toughness by our team," Brady said "We're going to remember this one for the rest of our lives."

CHAPTER 2

AFL ROOTS, NFL CHAMPS

The New England Patriots didn't suddenly appear on the NFL map and begin winning. In fact, they weren't even called the New England Patriots for their first 11 seasons. The Boston Patriots were charter members of the American Football League (AFL) when it was founded in 1960 as a rival league to the NFL.

Early on, the AFL didn't have anywhere close to the amount of talent on display in the NFL.

Gino Cappelletti starred at wide receiver and kicker for the early Boston Patriots teams.

The Patriots moved into sprawling Schaefer Stadium before the 1971 season.

But the AFL teams built up their rosters. They got a boost when the league signed a national television contract with NBC, putting it on equal footing with the NFL. And AFL owners weren't afraid to spend money. They went hard after top college players, and they also signed away some stars from the NFL.

Those first Patriots teams had such standouts as running back Jim Nance, receiver/placekicker Gino Cappelletti, linebacker Nick Buoniconti, and defensive lineman Jim Hunt.

They went 9–4–1 in their second year and again in their third, and took the AFL Eastern Division in 1963 by beating the Buffalo Bills in a playoff. However, Boston lost to the San Diego Chargers in the AFL Championship Game. That was the closest the Patriots would come to a title for another 32 years.

They didn't have a true home field, either. In their first three seasons, the Patriots played at Boston University's Nickerson Field. Then they played six seasons at Fenway Park, the city's famous baseball stadium. Then followed one year at Boston College's Alumni Stadium and one season at Harvard Stadium.

Finally, in 1971, Schaefer Stadium opened in Foxborough, Massachusetts, approximately halfway between Boston and Providence, Rhode Island. Team owners changed the name to the New England Patriots to reflect their more regional fan base.

CALL TO THE HALL

Seven former Patriots are in the Pro Football Hall of Fame, an honor Tom Brady and Bill Belichick also are likely to receive. Those already honored are linebackers Nick Buoniconti (1962–68), Andre Tippett (1982–93), and Junior Seau (2006–09); guard John Hannah (1973–85); cornerback Mike Haynes (1976–82); running back Curtis Martin (1995–97); and former head coach Bill Parcells (1993–96).

Unfortunately the team's name didn't have much effect on how it played. Starting in 1967, the Patriots went nine years without posting a winning record. They finally returned to the playoffs in 1976. It took them another nine years to get really good.

They made the AFC playoffs as a wild-card team in 1985. Then the Patriots beat the New York Jets, the Los Angeles Raiders, and the Miami Dolphins—all on the road—to reach the Super Bowl. The Chicago Bears, who had perhaps the most feared and physical defense pro football has ever seen, awaited them in New Orleans.

The Patriots lost 46–10, but they were becoming a quality team. They had a winning record the next three years before slipping again. But the tough times didn't last long, thanks in part to two men who didn't wear a uniform on Sundays.

Bill Parcells, who had won two Super Bowls with the New York Giants, was hired as head coach in 1993. He drafted Drew Bledsoe with the first overall pick that year, saying the Patriots had found their franchise quarterback.

The next year, Robert Kraft bought the team. Kraft was a lifelong Patriots fan and season ticket holder who stepped in

Bill Parcells, *left*, and Drew Bledsoe led the Patriots to the Super Bowl, but they couldn't bring the Lombardi Trophy back to New England with them.

when it looked like the franchise might be moved away from New England.

In his fourth season with the Patriots, Parcells guided Kraft's club to the Super Bowl. New England lost to the Green Bay Packers, and Parcells soon left to coach the New York Jets.

But the Patriots had become a regular in the playoffs. In 2000 Kraft hired Bill Belichick as head coach. They drafted Brady the same year. It was time to launch the dynasty.

CHAPTER 3

KRAFT, BRADY, AND BELICHICK

Robert Kraft had already been through two head coaches by 2000. Bill Parcells forced his way out of New England to join the New York Jets in 1997. Pete Carroll then spent three seasons in charge of the Patriots.

Kraft fired Carroll after the Patriots went 8–8 in 1999. He decided to hire Bill Belichick as Carroll's replacement, even though several other NFL owners had warned Kraft to stay away. Belichick had flopped in the same role with the

Robert Kraft, *left*, and Bill Belichick chat on the sidelines before the Patriots' first preseason game in 2000.

Cleveland Browns from 1991 through 1995, going 37–45 and making a lot of enemies with his gruff demeanor in Cleveland. He was even called "Dr. Evil" by some.

But Kraft knew Belichick had a brilliant mind for defense. He had won Super Bowls as a defensive assistant with the Giants under Parcells in 1986 and 1990. Kraft was a successful businessman, too. He recognized that someone doesn't have to be liked to be a success—respected, yes, but not necessarily liked.

SLOW START

In the first year of Belichick's reign in Foxborough, the Patriots went 5–11. They had the worst offense in the AFC East Division. They also had a sixth-round draft choice named Tom Brady. Selected No. 199 overall out of the University of Michigan, Brady sat behind Drew Bledsoe that first year. He appeared in one game, throwing three passes and completing one.

Not many people expected much from the Patriots—or Brady—in 2001, either. But in their second game of the season, Brady got his chance. Bledsoe rolled out to his right to pass and was hit hard by New York Jets linebacker Mo Lewis. The Patriots quarterback suffered a serious chest injury.

An injured Bledsoe, *right*, took on a mentorship role when Brady became the starter during the 2001 season.

"It was the loudest hit I could ever remember hearing," Brady said.

Onto the field stepped Brady. New England lost the game, but the Patriots would not lose many more that season, or in any season with Kraft, Belichick, and Brady.

Throughout the entire run of their dynasty, the Patriots have had only two placekickers. Adam Vinatieri's field goals were the difference in New England's first three Super Bowl wins. He left as a free agent for Indianapolis in 2006 and was replaced by Stephen Gostkowski. Through 2016 Gostkowski had led the NFL in scoring five times.

Kraft has taken his franchise from the valley to the mountaintop. He is also a powerful owner within the NFL. Belichick has more Super Bowl rings than any head coach.

As for Brady, many call him the greatest quarterback of all time, and it's hard to argue with that. A four-time Super Bowl MVP, Brady also owns two regular-season MVP awards. The player who slipped to the sixth round of the draft became the measuring stick for all quarterbacks.

SUPPORTING CAST

Although Kraft, Belichick, and Brady are the key figures in the Patriots' dynasty, many others made key contributions. Wide receiver Deion Branch was the only Patriot other than Brady to be named Super Bowl MVP. Offensive linemen Matt Light and Logan Mankins were two of the great blockers in Patriots history. Troy Brown was one of Brady's favorite targets as a

Deion Branch makes a play against the Philadelphia Eagles during his Super Bowl MVP performance in February 2005.

wide receiver, and when the Patriots were shorthanded in the secondary, he stepped in at defensive back. Running back Kevin Faulk was a versatile runner, receiver, blocker, and team leader.

Linebacker Mike Vrabel made a habit of catching touchdown passes from Brady when he was used on offense in the red zone. Defensive lineman Richard Seymour dominated up and down the line of scrimmage. Defensive backs Ty Law and Rodney Harrison were two of the hardest hitters at their positions the NFL has seen.

Linebacker Tedy Bruschi returned from a stroke at age 31 to be NFL Comeback Player of the Year in 2005. Defensive tackle Vince Wilfork was an immovable object in the middle of the line.

Wes Welker and Julian Edelman were both excellent punt returners in addition to being outstanding slot receivers. And don't forget Rob Gronkowski, the outrageous tight end who became one of the top end zone receiving threats in the league. They all contributed in different ways to different parts of one of the NFL's greatest dynasties.

CHAPTER 4

THE LOMBARDI
TROPHIES

When the Patriots opened the 2017 season, their fans celebrated their recent Super Bowl title. A championship banner was raised next to the video board in Gillette Stadium. Stars of past teams walked out with replicas of the Lombardi Trophy, the award for winning the Super Bowl. The Patriots had won five of them in seven tries since 2001.

The Patriots hold a ceremony at Gillette Stadium
in 2017 to celebrate their fifth Super Bowl title.

"In the end, you need to have great players, great chemistry, and you need to have great coaching," owner Robert Kraft said. "That's the formula."

Excitement has been the common thread for all eight of the Patriots' Super Bowls since 2001. Each of the games came down to the final seconds.

Those final seconds were painful for the Patriots and their fans three times. The others were happy endings. The biggest surprise came in the first of those seven Super Bowls, in February 2002 against the St. Louis Rams in New Orleans.

UPSET SPECIAL

The game looked like a mismatch. Known as "the Greatest Show on Turf," the Rams' high-powered offense looked unstoppable. Quarterback Kurt Warner was that season's NFL MVP. Running back Marshall Faulk was the NFL Offensive Player of the Year. Isaac Bruce and Torry Holt were as good as any pair of wide receivers in the sport.

New England had a young squad, and Brady had not even been starting for a full season. The Patriots were more of a defense-first, run-oriented team.

Ty Law picks off a Kurt Warner pass and returns it 47 yards for a touchdown in New England's first Super Bowl victory.

Yet New England led 17–3 after three quarters. The defense hit hard and often, especially against Bruce and Holt. But Warner rallied the Rams as he ran for one touchdown and passed for another. At 17–17 with 1:30 left, would Belichick play for overtime? Or would he trust his young quarterback in such a tight spot?

Belichick let Brady take a shot at winning the game. Relying on a series of quick, short passes, Brady marched the Patriots 53 yards. Then Adam Vinatieri made a 48-yard field goal on the final play. For the first time, New England was the NFL champion.

"I think that about every close game we had a chance to win, we won," Vinatieri said after the game. "I think when we were 0–2, everybody wrote us off except for the members of this team. We got on a streak and we just kept going."

Two years later, the Patriots were going back, this time facing the Carolina Panthers. In a strange game—no points were scored in the first or third quarters—the Panthers tied it 29–29 with 1:08 to go.

After a poor kickoff, Brady got New England in position for Vinatieri to do it all over again, this time from 41 yards. Championship number two was in the books.

The Patriots were back the next season, too. Only the Dallas Cowboys (after the 1992, 1993, and 1995 seasons) had

Adam Vinatieri watches his Super Bowl–winning field goal sail through the uprights against the Carolina Panthers.

won three Super Bowls in four years. If the Patriots could beat the Philadelphia Eagles, they would match that feat, and the word dynasty would begin to be tossed around in relation to the team.

They got it done. The margin of victory again was a field goal by Vinatieri as New England beat Philadelphia 24–21.

Randy Moss (81) and the Patriots let a perfect season slip through their fingers when the Giants pulled off an upset in the Super Bowl.

ALMOST PERFECT

None of those teams, however, compared to the 2007 Patriots. They went 16–0 in the regular season. Brady set an NFL record with 50 touchdown passes. Randy Moss caught 23 of them, also a record. They scored 589 points, which was 134 more than any other team that year. Then they won two playoff games to roll into the Super Bowl with a spotless 18–0 record.

But the New York Giants, only 10–6 during the season, shocked the football world. They prevented the Patriots from becoming only the second undefeated champion in the Super Bowl era with a 17–14 stunner of a victory.

It didn't get any better in New England's next trip to the big game. The Patriots again lost to the Giants, 21–17, after the 2011 season. So the Pats were on a Super Bowl losing streak

KILLER GIANTS

Quarterback Eli Manning made game-changing plays in the final minutes of both of New England's Super Bowl losses to the New York Giants. In the first one, Manning spun away from a heavy pass rush and lofted the ball in the direction of receiver David Tyree. With safety Rodney Harrison all over him, Tyree pinned the pass against his helmet before falling to the ground at the Patriots 24-yard line. Shortly after that 32-yard gain, Manning hit receiver Plaxico Burress in the end zone to win it.

Four years later, down 17–15, Manning connected with Mario Manningham against tight double coverage for a 38-yard gain. That moved the ball to midfield, and Ahmad Bradshaw capped the 88-yard drive with the winning touchdown run from 6 yards out with 57 seconds to play.

when they returned to it after the 2014 season. They faced the defending champions, the Seattle Seahawks.

Thanks to a tough-to-move defense and balanced offense, the Seahawks led 24–14 after three periods. Then Brady sparked what was at the time the biggest fourth-quarter comeback in Super Bowl history. His third touchdown pass pulled New England to within three points. Then he connected with Julian Edelman for the go-ahead score.

The Seahawks drove to the Patriots 1-yard line in the final seconds. But Patriots rookie cornerback Malcolm Butler came up with a game-saving interception, and Super Bowl trophy number four was soon in Brady's hands.

After the stunning comeback win over Atlanta in February 2017, the Patriots were back in the Super Bowl a year later. This time, however, the Eagles got revenge with a thrilling 41–33 victory. The game wasn't over until Brady's last-gasp pass fell incomplete in the end zone.

CHAPTER 5

AFTERMATH

T he NFL has had many dynasties through the years. From 1940 to 1947, the Chicago Bears won four championships. In the 1950s, the Detroit Lions won three in six seasons. So did the Cleveland Browns, who had also won all four titles in the All-America Football Conference before it folded.

The Green Bay Packers under Vince Lombardi—yes, the man for whom the Super Bowl trophy is named—were the dominant

Offensive coordinator Josh McDaniels, *right*, could be the next Patriots head coach once Belichick retires.

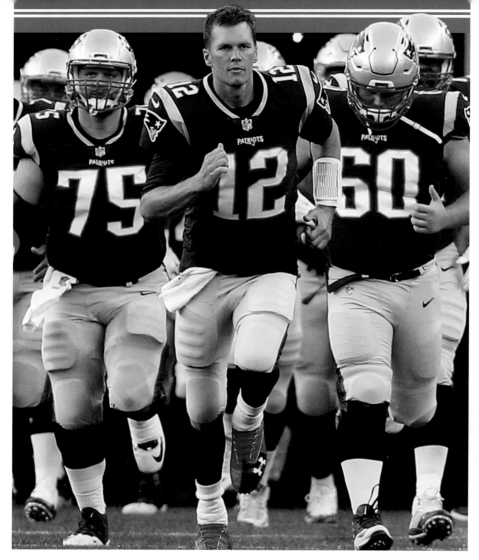

Brady has said he wants to keep leading the Patriots onto the field until he's 45 years old.

team of the 1960s, winning five titles. In the 1970s, the Pittsburgh Steelers won four times in six years. Then came the San Francisco 49ers, a four-time champion in the 1980s. Finally the Dallas Cowboys won three Super Bowls in four seasons in the '90s.

The Patriots have been the team of the 21st century, with five Super Bowl wins in eight tries. Can it last? Probably not. The key to those titles is quarterback Tom Brady. He turned 40 years old in 2017. Very few quarterbacks have remained at the top of their game beyond age 40. None that old have won a league championship.

That's not to say Brady won't be the first to do it. He already has broken new ground in so many ways. He believes he can play well until he is 45 or older. He showed that he had plenty left in the tank in February 2018. Brady broke his own record for most passing yards in a Super Bowl with 505 in their loss to the Eagles.

Still, it's unlikely that owner Robert Kraft and coach Bill Belichick will find another Brady. The Patriots will find other good quarterbacks—maybe even a few great ones. But no one could expect them to do what Brady has done.

A PACKAGE DEAL

Many NFL observers believe that when Brady retires, Belichick will also leave the NFL. Many of Belichick's top assistant coaches over the years have gone on to become head coaches elsewhere. Defensive coordinator Matt Patricia left

New England to become the head coach of the Detroit Lions in 2018. Meanwhile, offensive coordinator Josh McDaniels turned down a head coaching offer from the Indianapolis Colts. Many observers think McDaniels will be the man to replace Belichick eventually.

The strength of New England's coaching is how the team puts players in position to succeed. The Patriots don't ask their players to do anything that doesn't fit their skills. Instead they find what works best for each person, and they make sure to use those talents.

Ownership is an important part of winning, too. Kraft's son, Jonathan, is in position to run the team when his dad no

COURTING CONTROVERSY

The Patriots couldn't be more popular in New England. But they have made their share of enemies everywhere else. Fans of other teams haven't forgotten the various controversies that dogged the team in the Brady-Belichick era. The most infamous came early in the 2007 season. The New York Jets caught the Patriots illegally videotaping their signals on the sideline. Belichick was fined $500,000 for his role in "Spygate," while the Patriots were docked $250,000 and a first-round draft pick. It also led to speculation that the Patriots had done the same thing to get a leg up on other opponents.

From left, Robert Kraft, Rob Gronkowski, Brady, James White, and Dion Lewis each carry a Super Bowl trophy as the Patriots are honored by the Boston Red Sox at Fenway Park on April 3, 2017.

longer does. Like his father, Jonathan Kraft is well respected throughout pro football.

But predicting who will be the future stars in New England is impossible. Not many would have guessed that in 2000, when Brady was selected near the bottom of the draft, the Patriots had found the greatest winner the quarterback position has ever seen.

NEW ENGLAND PATRIOTS

SPAN OF DYNASTY

- 2001 to present

SUPER BOWLS WON

- 5 (2001, 2003, 2004, 2014, and 2016 seasons)

SUPER BOWLS LOST

- 2 (2007 and 2011 seasons)

AFC EAST TITLES WON

- 14 (2001, 2003–07, 2009–16)

REGULAR-SEASON RECORD

- 196–60

PLAYOFFS RECORD

- 25–9

KEY RIVALS

- New York Jets, Pittsburgh Steelers, Denver Broncos, Indianapolis Colts

INDIVIDUAL AWARDS

NFL MVP

- Tom Brady (2007, 2010)

SUPER BOWL MVP

- Tom Brady (2001, 2003, 2014, 2016 seasons)
- Deion Branch (2004)

OFFENSIVE PLAYER OF THE YEAR

- Tom Brady (2007, 2010)

COMEBACK PLAYER OF THE YEAR

- Tedy Bruschi (2005)
- Rob Gronkowski (2014)

DEFENSIVE ROOKIE OF THE YEAR

- Jerod Mayo (2008)

COACH OF THE YEAR

- Bill Belichick (2007, 2010)

JANUARY 27, 2000

Bill Belichick is hired as the Patriots' head coach.

SEPTEMBER 23, 2001

Starting quarterback Drew Bledsoe gets hurt in Game 2. Tom Brady takes over and leads the Patriots to the playoffs.

FEBRUARY 3, 2002

The Patriots win their first Super Bowl title with an upset of the St. Louis Rams.

FEBRUARY 1, 2004

The Patriots beat Carolina 32–29, winning their second NFL title on Adam Vinatieri's field goal as time expires.

FEBRUARY 6, 2005

The Patriots edge Philadelphia 24–21, repeating as Super Bowl champions.

FEBRUARY 3, 2008

New England's bid for an undefeated season ends with a shocking 17–14 loss to the New York Giants.

FEBRUARY 5, 2012

The Giants again defeat the Patriots in a tight Super Bowl, 21–17.

FEBRUARY 1, 2015

Malcolm Butler's interception in the final seconds versus Seattle clinches New England's fourth Super Bowl crown.

FEBRUARY 5, 2017

An epic comeback from 25 points down leads to the first overtime in Super Bowl history. The Patriots finish the comeback with a 34–28 defeat of the Atlanta Falcons.

FEBRUARY 4, 2018

The Eagles come back in the final 3 minutes to defeat the Patriots 41–33 in a thrilling Super Bowl.

GLOSSARY

COORDINATOR
An assistant coach who is in charge of the offense or defense.

DEFLATE
To take air out of something that has been inflated, such as a balloon or a football.

DYNASTY
A team that has an extended period of success, usually winning multiple championships in the process.

LINE OF SCRIMMAGE
The place on the field where a play starts.

OVERTIME
An extra period of play when the score is tied after regulation.

RED ZONE
The area between an opponent's 20-yard line and the goal line.

REPLICA
A copy, not the original.

RIVAL
An opponent with whom a player or team has a fierce and ongoing competition.

SACK
A tackle of the quarterback behind the line of scrimmage before he can pass the ball.

TWO-POINT CONVERSION
An option for teams that have scored a touchdown to try a running or passing play from the 2-yard line for two points, instead of kicking for one point.

VERSATILE
Able to do many different things.

ONLINE RESOURCES

Booklinks
NONFICTION NETWORK
FREE! ONLINE NONFICTION RESOURCES

To learn more about Tom Brady and the New England Patriots, visit abdobooklinks.com. These links are routinely monitored and updated to provide the most current information available.

BOOKS

Gordon, Nick. *Tom Brady*. Minneapolis, MN: Abdo Publishing, 2016.

Scheff, Matt. *New England Patriots*. Minneapolis, MN: Abdo Publishing, 2017.

Wilner, Barry. *Total Football*. Minneapolis, MN: Abdo Publishing, 2017.

MORE INFORMATION

INDEX

ABOUT THE AUTHOR

Barry Wilner has been a sportswriter for the Associated Press since 1976 and has covered the Super Bowl, the Olympics, the World Cup, the Stanley Cup Finals, and many other major sports events. He has written more than 60 books. He lives in Garnerville, New York.